A Little Person Like You
Whose Mommy Goes to Prison

A Little Person Like You

Whose Mommy Goes to Prison

Patty Prewitt

Pictures by Yellow Moon

Published by Some People Press
PO Box 12453, Portland, Oregon 97212

ISBN: 979-8-9941977-0-7

Cover and book design by Laura Glazer
Editing by Harrell Fletcher
Proofreading by Gretchen Dykstra

www.somepeoplepress.com
@somepeoplepress

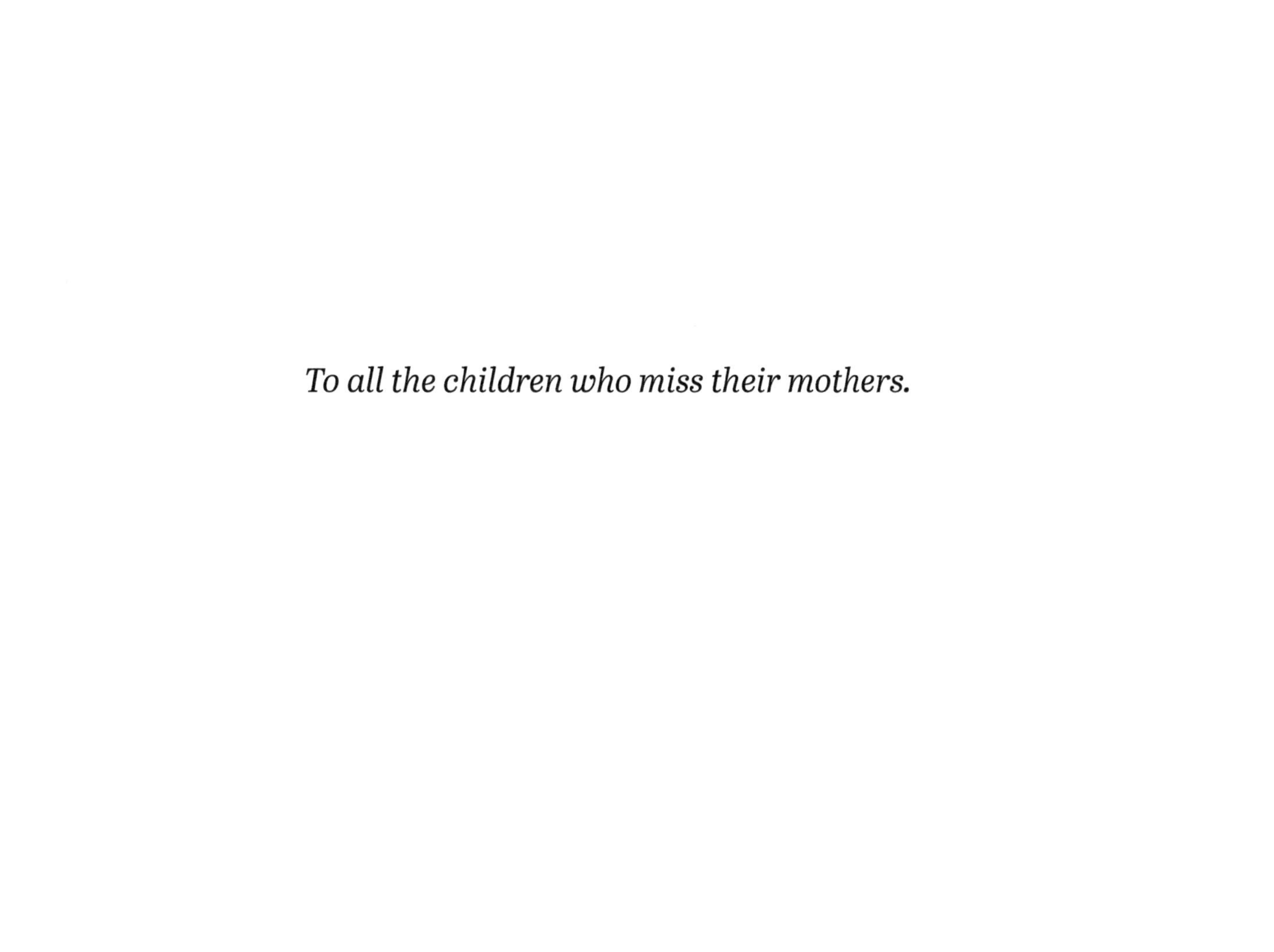

To all the children who miss their mothers.

Once there was a little girl
or maybe a little boy.

It really doesn't matter, because this Little Person was just like you.

This Little Person loved
Mommy so much and played
with Mommy as much as possible.

They played outside.

They played inside.

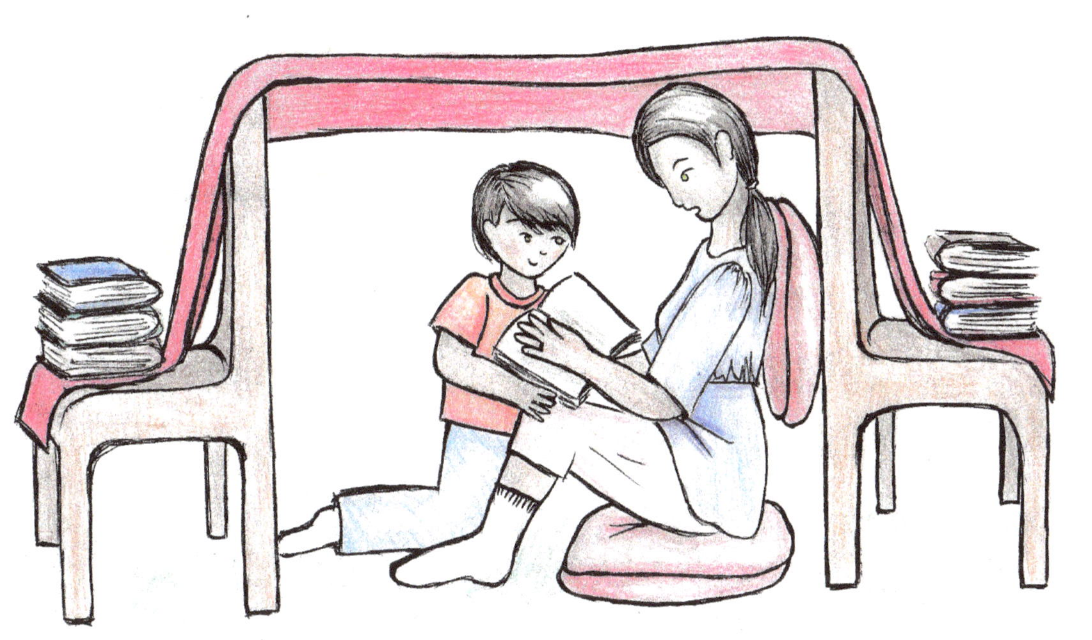

They played with their dog.

They tried to play with their cat,
but the cat had other ideas.

Cats can be like that.

Z Z
z

Mommy read stories to this Little Person and tucked this Little Person into bed, snug as a bug in a rug.

One night Mommy sat this Little Person down and with a sad face told this Little Person that Mommy was going to have to go away for a while.

Mommy said she had to go to Big Person
time-out. This Little Person had been
in Little Person time-out before
and tried to understand.

Mommy said the Big Person
time-out is far away in a place
called prison.

This Little Person clung
to Mommy and cried and cried.
This Little Person didn't
want Mommy to leave.

Mommy didn't want to leave
this Little Person, but there
was no way out of this.

Mommy had to leave this Little Person

to go to Big Person time-out.

This Little Person missed
Mommy every day,

but this Little Person drew
pictures for Mommy and...

...talked to her on the phone, too.

On special days this Little Person
got to go to the prison and not only
see Mommy but hug and kiss her, too.

Those were the best days, until time
was up and this Little Person had
to leave Mommy behind in prison.
Those goodbyes were awful.
This Little Person cried and cried.

One day this Little Person heard
that Mommy was coming home
and got so excited!

This Little Person
jumped in the kitchen,
jumped in the living room,
and jumped outside.

This Little Person had been
waiting and waiting and waiting
for the Big Person time-out
to be done and over.

Mommy was coming HOME!

Mommy came home to her
Little Person and they hugged and hugged
and cried tears of happiness.

They were very happy
to be back together.

B
N
MOMMY
Me

Mommy promised
to try every day
to never leave this
Little Person again.

In the United States, nearly 150,000 mothers are incarcerated in prisons, leaving an estimated 1.3 million minors separated from their primary caregivers. Over 2,019,900 women are jailed in the U.S. every year, and 80 percent are mothers.

These millions of innocent children are cruelly torn from their support and are punished harshly. Some end up with families who may be ill-prepared to care for additional children. Some children end up in the bureaucratic foster care system. Some of them end up in juvenile detention. None are unscarred. The overwhelming number of children abandoned due to maternal incarceration end up behind bars.

Remember that these children are innocent victims. I beseech you to bring kindness and understanding to these wounded children and their mothers.

My children were 16, 14, 12, 10, and 8 when I was sent
to prison for a crime I didn't commit. During my
nearly 40 years of incarceration, I met thousands
of heartbroken mothers. I wrote this book for all
our children and the trauma they experienced.
Kids need to know they are not alone, and that their
mothers love them with all their hearts.

—Patty Prewitt, Jane's mom

Patty and her daughter Jane.

I was 16 when my mother was incarcerated.
My younger siblings and I didn't know anyone in
prison. A book like this could have helped us not
feel so alone and given us hope that eventually we
would have our happy ending. And we finally did.

—Jane Watkins, Patty's daughter

About the author

Patty Prewitt went to prison in 1986 for a murder she did not commit. She and her people fought for justice every day of her incarceration. She was freed by the governor on December 20, 2024. She hit the ground running. Her book, *Trying to Catch Lightning in a Jar*, chronicling the first 20 years of her incarceration, was published just months later by Some People Press. Prewitt is finishing her bachelor's degree at Washington University St Louis and writing another book about the second half of her imprisonment. She's living happily and free near Kansas City, Missouri, with her oldest daughter.

About the artist

Yellow Moon has served 10 years in a Missouri prison, where they are a student with the Washington University Prison Education Project and an active member of Prison Performing Arts.

About the publisher

Some People Press publishes autobiographies by formerly incarcerated writers, as well as books on art and other subjects. We challenge the idea that only certain people—with the right education, experiences, and connections—can be published authors. Instead, we encourage writers to use their existing skills and to write about what they know best, their own lives. All profits from sales of autobiographies are split evenly between the press and the author. Some People Press is supported by book sales and contributions via Venmo @somepeoplepress.